# 20 THINGS YOU DIDN'T KNOW ABOUT STICK BUGS

DID YOU KNOW? BUGS



DOUG BRADLEY

PowerKiDS press

Published in 2027 by The Rosen Publishing Group, Inc.
2544 Clinton Street, Buffalo, NY 14224



Portions of this work were originally authored by Heather Moore Niver and published as *20 Fun Facts About Stick Bugs*. All new material in this edition was authored by Doug Bradley.

Editor: Greg Roza
Book Design: Michael Flynn

Photo Credits: Cover Wuttipon/Shutterstock.com; series background freshcare/Shutterstock.com; p. 4 Knorre/Shutterstock.com; p. 5 https://commons.wikimedia.org/wiki/File:Acrophylla_alta_Holotype_female_in_nature.jpg; p. 6 Ava Peattie/Shutterstock.com; p. 7 Mark Brandon/Shutterstock.com; p. 8 MyTravelCurator/Shutterstock.com; pp. 9, 21 Eric Isselee/Shutterstock.com; p. 10 Ratchanee Sawasdijira/Shutterstock.com; p. 11 Fahmi Ezudeen Bin Azhar/Shutterstock.com; p. 12 Paolo Pako/Shutterstock.com; p. 13 Danny Ye/Shutterstock.com; p. 14 Vladimir Wrangel/Shutterstock.com; p. 15 Ray Wilson/Alamy; p. 16 Milan Zygmunt/Shutterstock.com; p. 17 Mark Brandon/Shutterstock.com; p. 18 zaidi razak/Shutterstock.com; p. 19 Yusia13/Shutterstock.com; p. 20 SIMON SHIM/Shutterstock.com; p. 22 Fabrizio Misson/Shutterstock.com; p. 23 Knorre/Shutterstock.com; p. 24 Insectpedia/Shutterstock.com; p. 25 Space creator/Shutterstock.com; p. 26 Mark Brandon/Shutterstock.com; p. 27 kurt_G/Shutterstock.com; p. 29 CinemaPhoto/Shutterstock.com.

Cataloging-in-Publication Data

Names: Bradley, Doug, 1971-.
Title: 20 things you didn't know about stick bugs / Doug Bradley.
Description: Buffalo, New York : PowerKids Press, 2027. | Series: Did you know? bugs | Includes glossary and index.
Identifiers: ISBN 9781499457483 (pbk.) | ISBN 9781499457490 (library bound) | ISBN 9781499457506 (ebook)
Subjects: LCSH: Stick insects–Juvenile literature.
Classification: LCC QL509.5 B656 2027 | DDC 595.729–dc23

Printed in China

Some of the images in this book illustrate individuals who are models. The depictions do not imply actual situations or events.

CPSIA Compliance Information: Batch #QSPK27. For Further Information contact Rosen Publishing at 1-800-237-9932.

# CONTENTS

# INSECTS IN DISGUISE

Stick bugs are sometimes called stick insects or walking sticks. They're true masters of **disguise**! These creepers look like plant parts, which helps **camouflage** them so they can hide from **predators**.

Stick bugs and leaf insects are both part of the order, or group, called phasmids (FAZ-muhdz). "Phasmid" comes from the Greek word for "ghost," which describes this hard-to-see bug pretty well. Still, scientists have spotted nearly 3,500 different **species** of stick bugs, and they expect to find more species in the coming years.

In November 2024, a new stick bug species was discovered living high up in the trees of a rainforest of northeastern Australia. Scientists think it might be the heaviest stick bug on record, weighing up to 1.6 ounces (45.4 gr).

# STICK BUG BODY

## FACT 1

## STICK BUG BODIES HAVE THREE DIFFERENT PARTS.

Like all insects, stick bugs have a head, thorax, and abdomen. The head contains its brain and mouth. Three pairs of legs are attached to its thorax. So are wings if the stick bug has them. The stick bug's abdomen holds several **organs**, such as its stomach.

The Indian stick bug is one of the most common stick bugs in the world.

2 FEELERS
HEAD
THORAX
ABDOMEN
6 LONG LEGS

## FACT 2

## SOME STICK BUGS HAVE COLORS AND PATTERNS ON THEIR BODIES.

Most stick bugs are brown, which allows them to hide in trees. However, stick bugs come in many other colors. They can also be green, black, gray, or even blue. These colors help them hide against moss, leaves, and even flowers.

Some stick bugs look just like moss or tree bark.

Stick bugs with colorful wings are sometimes called jeweled stick bugs.

## FACT 3

## SOME STICK BUGS USE THEIR WINGS FOR MORE THAN FLYING.

Some stick bug species have bright wings. They may use them to escape from predators. When a predator is nearby they quickly unfold their wings, then drop to the ground and hide their wings. The predator looks all over for the bright wings while the stick bug hides among leaves and sticks.

# STICK BUG LIFESTYLE

## FACT 4

## STICK BUGS AREN'T SHY.

Stick bugs can easily hide in sticks and leaves, but most of them hang out in the open. They stay so still that they're unlikely to be noticed. When they move, stick bugs sway, or slowly move back and forth, to make it look like they're a stick blowing in the breeze.

Although they may be hard to spot in the wild, most stick bugs can be handled gently when you do find them.

It can be almost impossible to find a stick bug resting on a forest floor. Can you see the stick bug?

## FACT 5

## YOU'RE MOST LIKELY TO SEE A STICK BUG AT NIGHT.

Stick bugs stay up all night long. That's because they're nocturnal animals, meaning they're most active at night. During the day, they hide under leaves and plants to avoid becoming a meal to larger predators.

# BIG STICKS!

## FACT 6

## THE BIGGEST STICK BUG IS NICKNAMED THE "MEGASTICK."

The littlest walking sticks are about 0.5 inch (1.3 cm) long, but not all stick bugs are tiny. The biggest walking sticks are close to 13 inches (33 cm) long. When they stretch out their legs, they can reach 21 inches (53 cm)!

The island nation of Borneo is home to many species of stick bugs, including Chan's megastick. The largest megastick on record was 22.3 inches (56.7 cm) long with its legs fully stretched out.

Scientists today think the tree lobster is one of, if not the rarest insect species in the world. They are only found on Lord Howe Island near Australia.

## THE "TREE LOBSTER" STICK BUG IS SO BIG THAT IT'S MUCH EASIER TO SPOT THAN OTHER STICK BUGS.

## FACT 7

For 80 years, scientists thought that a flightless stick insect called a tree lobster was **extinct**. It was commonly used to catch fish. But in 2001, they found some on an island near Australia. Tree lobsters get their name because their thick, hard **exoskeleton** looks much like a lobster's.

# SURVIVAL SKILLS

## FACT 8

## STICK BUGS SHOULDN'T BE CONFUSED WITH STINKBUGS, BUT SOME CAN GET SMELLY.

Some stick bugs make themselves stink so predators won't want to eat them. They might spray a stinky brown liquid to keep from being eaten. The American walking stick can squirt a fluid that stings or blinds its predators for a while.

The spiny devil walking stick sprays a nasty brownish liquid to scare off predators.

This black butcherbird caught a stick bug to eat.

FACT 9

## YOUNG STICK BUGS MAY LOSE A LEG TO ESCAPE A PREDATOR.

Mice, birds, reptiles, spiders, and bats all enjoy a nice stick bug for dinner. But young stick bugs have an interesting way of avoiding hungry predators. If a young stick bug is in danger, it can drop off one of its legs to escape a hungry predator. It can grow the leg back the next time it **molts**.

## FACT 10 SOME STICK BUGS PLAY DEAD TO ESCAPE PREDATORS.

When approached by hungry predators, some walking sticks pretend to be dead in hopes that the predator will pass them by. Others have sharp spines on their legs. When they're in danger, the stick bug can stab at the enemy.

This is a close-up of a thorny devil stick bug. The sharp spines can do a lot of damage to predators.

# STICK BUGS OF THE WORLD

| COMMON NAME | FUNKY FEATURES |
| --- | --- |
| INDIAN STICK INSECT | dark brown to bright green color |
| PINK-WING STICK INSECT | light brown with bright pink wings |
| THORNY DEVIL STICK INSECT | fast moving with spines on its legs |
| TITAN STICK INSECT | longest stick bug in Australia |
| SPUR-LEGGED PHASMID | males have wings, but females don't |
| LORD HOWE ISLAND STICK INSECT | also called the tree lobster |
| GOLIATH STICK INSECT | green with yellow spots; green wings |
| BIG-HEADED STICK INSECT | large head; small wings but doesn't fly |
| CROWN STICK INSECT | lumps on its head look like a crown |
| PEPPERMINT STICK INSECT | named for its minty smell |

# ALL ABOUT EGGS

## FACT 11

## FEMALE STICK BUGS CAN HAVE BABIES WITHOUT THE HELP OF MALE STICK BUGS.

Female stick bugs are some of the most independent women on the planet! They can have female babies without the help of a male walking stick. This is called parthenogenesis (pahr-thuh-noh-JEH-nuh-suhs). They lay eggs that **hatch** into clones, or exact copies of themselves.

This is a close-up of a female stick bug laying eggs.

This baby stick bug is coming out of its egg.

## THERE ARE FAR MORE FEMALE STICK BUGS THAN THERE ARE MALE STICK BUGS.

**FACT 12**

Stick bug mothers can **mate** with a male if they want to. This is the only time there's a chance that an egg will hatch a male. Female stick bugs are usually bigger than males and stronger than males.

## FACT 13

## FEMALES GET CREATIVE WHEN HIDING THEIR EGGS.

Many female stick bugs hide their eggs in soil or hollow plants to keep them safe from predators. Others glue them to the bottom of leaves. Some drop the eggs one at a time so predators don't find a large cluster of eggs to dine on.

Tiny stick bug eggs cling to the underside of a leaf.

The bump on a stick bug egg is called a capitulum.

## SOME KINDS OF STICK BUGS WANT ANTS TO STEAL THEIR EGGS.

**FACT 14**

Some stick bug species lay eggs with a special bump that ants like to snack on. The ants bring the eggs to their nest, eat the bump, and leave the rest. The eggs stay in their nest, safe from predators, until they hatch.

# LIL' STICK BUGS

## FACT 15

**BABY WALKING STICKS LOOK EXACTLY LIKE ADULT WALKING STICKS—EXCEPT SMALLER!**

In the insect world, many newborn bugs look like little worms called larvae. These tiny worms often go through a process of change that results in an adult bug. When a baby stick bug, called a nymph, breaks out of its egg, it looks just like its mother, but it's a lot smaller.

Baby stick bugs are tiny!

Molting is a dangerous time for stick bugs. They need to sit still while their new exoskeleton hardens, making them an easy target for predators.

## A WALKING STICK REPLACES ITS EXOSKELETON SEVERAL TIMES BEFORE IT BECOMES AN ADULT.

## FACT 16

When they hatch, young stick bugs don't have wings, but they can run around and climb. As they grow, they molt between 4 and 8 times. Females often molt one more time than males. Once they become adults, they have fully grown wings.

## FACT 17 MALE STICK BUGS ARE USUALLY BETTER FLIERS THAN FEMALE STICK BUGS.

Many male stick bugs have a full set of wings and can fly with no problem. However, females of the same species often have much smaller wings and much bigger bodies. So flying isn't as easy for females.

Not all species of stick bug have wings.

## LEAVES ARE A STICK BUG'S FAVORITE MEAL.

FACT 18

Most stick bug species live in warm areas. Some live in cooler parts of the planet, too. They like to live in forests and grasslands, which are full of the tasty leaves they like to eat. Walking sticks are herbivores, which means they only eat plants.

Stick bugs get most of the water they need to live from the leaves they eat.

## FACT 19

## IN A PINCH, STICK BUGS WILL EAT THEIR OWN SKIN.

Young stick bugs sometimes eat the old exoskeleton after they molt. It sounds gross, but this is a great way for the bugs to get healthy **nutrients**. Molting stick bugs don't eat, so the leftover skin makes the perfect meal for a hungry, growing stick bug.

By eating their skin, walking sticks also hide a sign of where they are from predators.

## STICK BUG POOP MAKES A MEAL FOR SOME OTHER BUGS.

## FACT 20

Stick bugs help smaller insects get the nutrients they need in a really weird way. They use their strong mouthparts, called mandibles, to chew and break down plant leaves. Their droppings contain plant material that other smaller insects feed on.

# WONDERFUL WALKING STICKS

Stick bugs may not be fast, but can still beat you in a game of hide-and-seek. Few animals hide as well as a stick bug, thanks to its body shape and coloring.

Stick bugs are some cool creepy crawlers you might want to check out. Some people even keep them as pets. However, if too many are removed from their natural homes as pets, the bugs could become extinct. We want these cool critters to live a long time!

Stick bugs pets are easy to take care of.

# GLOSSARY

**camouflage:** Colors or shapes in animals that allow them to blend with their surroundings.

**disguise:** An outward appearance that hides what something really is.

**exoskeleton:** The hard outer covering of an animal's body.

**extinct:** No longer living.

**hatch:** To break open or come out of.

**mate:** To come together to make babies.

**molt:** The act of shedding an exoskeleton that has become too small.

**nutrient:** Something a living thing needs to grow and stay alive.

**organ:** A part inside an animal's body.

**predator:** An animal that hunts other animals for food.

**species:** A group of plants or animals that are all of the same kind.

# FOR MORE INFORMATION

## BOOKS

Becker, Trudy. *Walking Sticks.* Mendota Heights, MN: North Star Editions, 2023.

Coghill, Dixon. *Caring for Your Stick Insects, Stick Bugs, and Leaf Insects as Pets*. Independently published, 2025.

## WEBSITES

**Australian Stick Insects**
*www.ozanimals.com/wildlife/Insect/Stick-Insects.html*
Learn more about the stick bugs of Australia with photos and details about many different species.

**Care of Stick Insects**
*australianmuseum.net.au/Care-of-Stick-Insects*
This is a great site to learn more about walking sticks with photos, facts, and maps.

Publisher's note to educators and parents: Our editors have carefully reviewed these websites to ensure that they are suitable for students. Many websites change frequently, however, and we cannot guarantee that a site's future contents will continue to meet our high standards of quality and educational value. Be advised that students should be closely supervised whenever they access the internet.

# INDEX